AUSTRALIA'S
SCARIEST
CREATURES

BY JOHN LESLEY

NASTY STINGERS

REDBACK publishing

First published 2024 by
Redback Publishing
PO Box 357 Frenchs Forest NSW 2086, Australia

www.redbackpublishing.com
orders@redbackpublishing.com

ISBN 978-1-761400-43-8

Author: John Lesley
Editor: Caroline Thomas
Designer: Redback Publishing
Original illustrations © Redback Publishing 2024
Originated by Redback Publishing

NATIONAL LIBRARY OF AUSTRALIA

A catalogue record for this book is available from the National Library of Australia

Acknowledgements
Abbreviations: l—left, r—right, b—bottom, t—top, c—centre, m—middle
We would like to thank the following for permission to reproduce photographs: Shutterstock; p4-5c Lisa-ann Gershwin, CC BY 4.0 <https://creativecommons.org/licenses/by/4.0>, via Wikimedia Commons; p4tc GondwanaGirl 04:29, 6 January 2009 (UTC), CC BY-SA 3.0 <https://creativecommons.org/licenses/by-sa/3.0>, via Wikimedia Commons; p10-11c Didier Descouens, CC BY-SA 3.0 <https://creativecommons.org/licenses/by-sa/3.0>, via Wikimedia Commons; p12tc Avispa marina.jpg: Guido Gautsch, Toyota, Japanderivative work: Mithril, CC BY-SA 2.0 <https://creativecommons.org/licenses/by-sa/2.0>, via Wikimedia Commons; p14-15c User:Amada44, CC BY 3.0 <https://creativecommons.org/licenses/by/3.0>, via Wikimedia Commons; p14br A. R. Mc Culloch, Public domain, via Wikimedia Commons; p16-17c Third Silence Nature Photography, CC BY 4.0 <https://creativecommons.org/licenses/by/4.0>, via Wikimedia Commons; p18br IG: divecycle, CC BY-SA 4.0 <https://creativecommons.org/licenses/by-sa/4.0>, via Wikimedia Commons; p19bl george_vaughan, CC0, via Wikimedia Commons

CONTENTS

Irukandji Jellyfish 4
Blue-ringed Octopus 6
Bluebottle 8
Cone Snail 10
Box Jellyfish 12
Short-tailed Stingray 14
Puffer Fish 16
Sea Snakes 18
Stonefish 20
Sea Anemone 22
Sponges 24
Stingers Around the World 26
How Dangerous Are They? 28
Safety in the Ocean 30
Glossary (Stingers Word List) 31
Index 32

IRUKANDJI JELLYFISH

Carukia barnesi

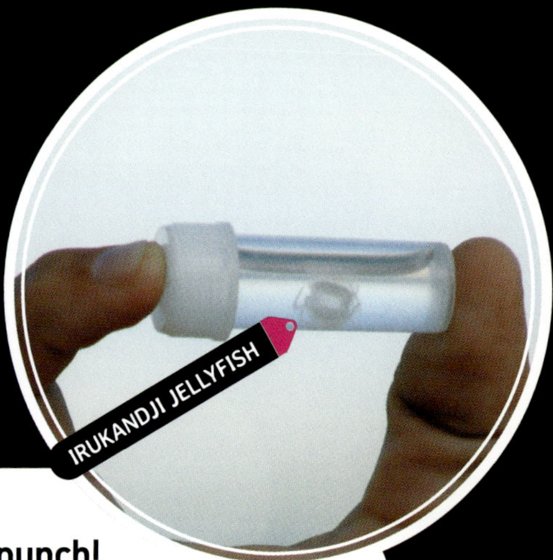

This tiny jellyfish packs a punch! At only two centimetres wide, and being see-through, Irukandji jellyfish are easy to miss if you are swimming, snorkelling or diving nearby. Their four stinging tentacles are almost invisible and can trail for up to half a metre in the water.

WHAT HAPPENS IF YOU ARE STUNG?

Irukandji toxin affects the brain and nervous system. Some people can get very sick, and the toxin can be fatal. Intense pain, nausea and difficulty breathing are common. This may occur within the first hour after being stung.

An Irukandji jellyfish stings by shooting poisoned arrows or barbs that are stored in tiny capsule-like cells called nematocysts. Once triggered by motion sensors, this tiny-arrow attack allows the Irukandji to quickly catch and immobilise prey. It then draws this fresh meal up into its mouth using its tentacles.

FACT

There's a good reason Irikandjis are also called 'stingers'!

FACT FILE

Length: bell about 2 cm wide
Tentacles: 4 tentacles up to 50 cm long
Colour: translucent
Poisonous: yes
Habitat: warm oceans
Scientific name: *Carukia barnesi*

FACT

The experts say you will feel a sense of 'impending doom' after being stung by an Irukandji. This condition is called Irukandji Syndrome.

AVOID BEING A VICTIM

1. Wear a full body suit.
2. Seek advice from experts.
3. Swim at beaches patrolled by lifeguards.
4. Don't touch an Irukandji. Even if it is dead on the beach, it can still sting.

WHERE DO THEY LIVE?

Irukandji live in the sea in warm and temperate regions around the world. There are more of them in Australian waters in summer and autumn, but they can still be present at other times. Australian scientists have been studying Irukandji in the waters of Queensland's Great Barrier Reef for many years.

BLUE-RINGED OCTOPUS

Hapalochlaena

The little blue-ringed octopus is a plain brown or sandy colour until it gets upset. Then bright blue circles appear all over its body. This is its warning signal to get back or it will bite.

BITE

The bite itself causes little pain, and some people do not realise they have been bitten until they start to feel very sick. This is the stage at which the octopus venom is starting to take effect and medical help is needed urgently.

VENOM

The octopus uses its venom to immobilise its food so that it can eat without the little fish or crustacean escaping. The venom is also useful for fighting off predators such as sharks and humans.

HUMAN CONTACT

Humans usually encounter a blue-ringed octopus when investigating rock pools, or when diving. The octopus can squeeze itself into a discarded shell or even a piece of human rubbish like a drink can.

FACT

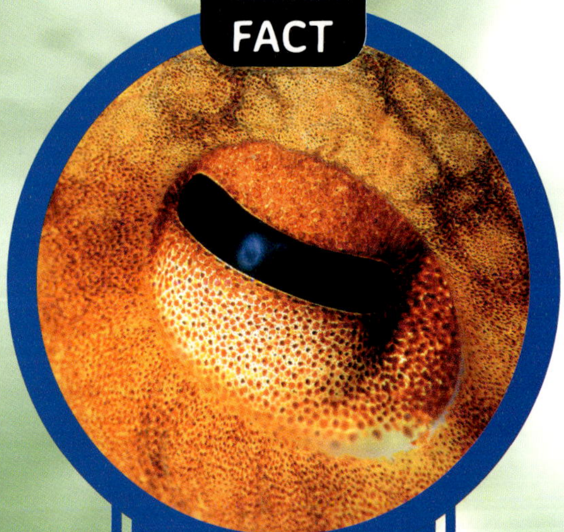

Octopuses have good eyesight, so they can see you coming!

FACT FILE

Length: body about 3 cm wide
Tentacles: 8 legs about 6 cm long
Colour: brown, sandy with blue rings
Poisonous: yes
Habitat: tropical regions of the Pacific Ocean
Scientific name: the four types of blue-ringed octopus are in the group called *Hapalochlaena*

FACT

The female guards her eggs until they hatch, which may take some months. Once the eggs hatch, the female dies.

BLUEBOTTLE

Physalia physalis

These creatures are a beautiful blue, and they look like discarded toys or balloons when they are washed up on the beach. There can be thousands of them dead on the sand after a storm, but don't touch any. They can still sting!

Each bluebottle looks like it is just a single animal, but it is actually made up of four different creatures all joined together as a colony. The blue bubble, the tentacles, the feeding, and the reproductive parts are all different creatures.

TENTACLES

Each bluebottle has one long tentacle covered in stingers. A tentacle that has broken off can float around in the ocean and wrap around a swimmer's leg or face. The stings are very, very painful.

GAS BUBBLE

The blue bubble traps gas so that this jellyfish can use the wind to move around on the surface of the ocean, while its stinging tentacle hangs below and catches food.

FACT

Australia's bluebottles are not the same as the Portuguese Man o' War, which is a larger but similar creature that lives in the Atlantic Ocean.

FACT

Many people who swim at Australia's beaches have been stung by a bluebottle.

FACT FILE

Length: body 3-5 cm
Tentacles: can grow to 3 m long
Colour: blue
Stingers: yes
Habitat: warm ocean water along the east and west of Australia in the Pacific and Indian Oceans
Scientific name: *Physalia physalis*

Bluebottles are related to corals

CONE SNAIL

Conus geographus

The cone snail has a beautiful shell, but inside it lives a highly poisonous mollusc. There are hundreds of different types of cone snails. The most dangerous one in Australia is *Conus geographus*.

POISON DARTS

Being a mollusc, the cone snail cannot move quickly to hunt fish to eat, but the development of its toxic venom makes up for the snail's slowness. The snail hunts by shooting poisonous darts at its prey or any human who gets too close. A poisoned fish will stop moving so that the snail can eat it, and a human can die from the effects of the poison.

FACT

Scientists are researching whether a cone snail's deadly venom could be turned into a life-saving medicine.

FACT FILE

Length: shell up to 15 cm long, but the foot of the mollusc can extend out much further

Colour: purple and brown patterns on the shell and body

Poison: lethal to humans

Habitat: oceans and seas of northern Australia and other tropical parts of the Indian and Pacific Oceans

Scientific name: *Conus geographus*

FACT

Shell collectors all want at least one cone shell in their collection, but never pick up a live cone shell from the ocean. They are all dangerous.

BOX JELLYFISH

Chironex fleckeri

The box jellyfish is one of the most dangerous creatures in the ocean. They live in the warm oceans along the coasts of Queensland, the Northern Territory and Western Australia. They are also found in warm seas in many other parts of the world, in shallow waters and even in river mouths. They are rarely in the open sea.

TENTACLES

They look like a translucent, white box, with stinging tentacles dangling three metres down from each corner. However, if you see a box jellyfish that does not seem to have tentacles, don't be fooled! They can also contract their tentacles into bundles only as big as a fist.

STINGER SEASON

November to May is called 'marine stinger season' in the northern, coastal parts of Australia. Swimming at that time is dangerous unless you are at a beach patrolled by lifeguards.

DIET

The box jellyfish uses its stinging tentacles to catch its food, which includes prawns and small fish.

FACT

The box jellyfish sting is more painful than that of an Irukandji.

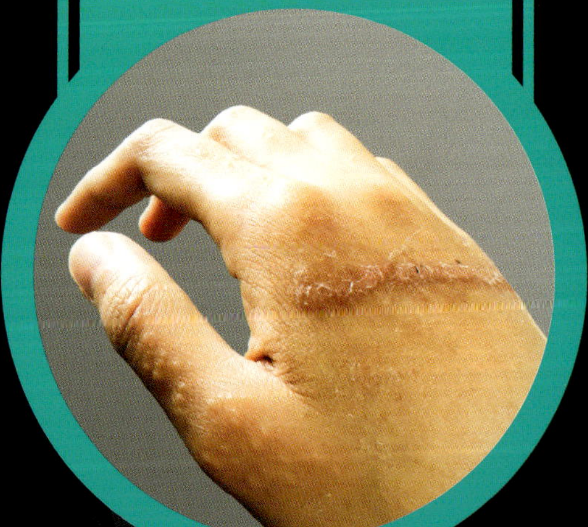

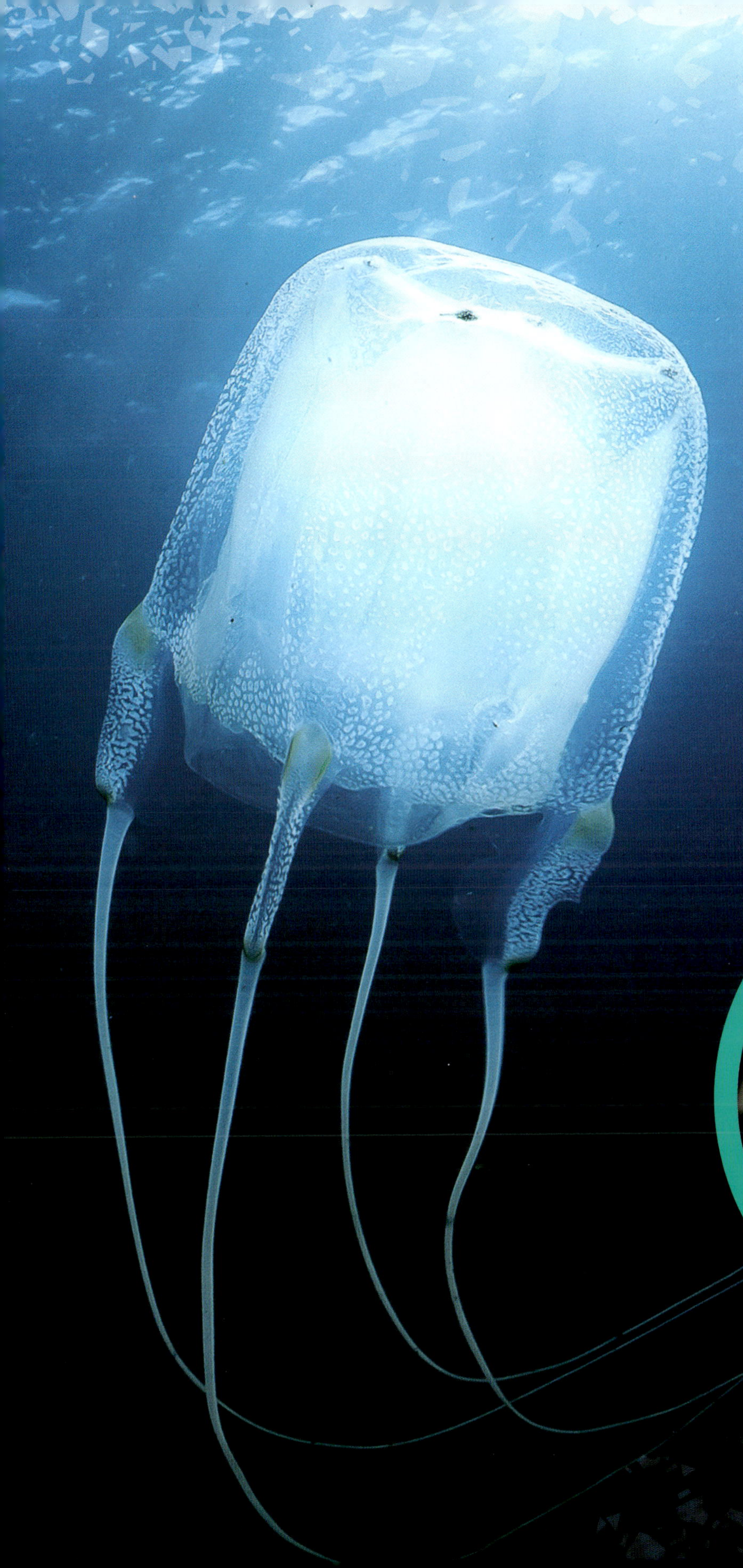

FACT FILE

Length: body about 40 cm wide, tentacles 3 m long

Tentacles: many tentacles with millions of stinging cells

Colour: translucent white

Poisonous: stings can be fatal to humans

Habitat: warm ocean waters

Scientific name: *Chironex fleckeri*

FACT

The box jellyfish is also called a sea wasp. Its tentacles leave a long line of stings across a person's skin.

SHORT-TAIL STINGRAY

Dasyatis brevicaudata

FACT

The cartilage of stingrays is the same type of tissue that humans have in the flexible parts of their ear and nose.

FACT

Famous naturalist, Steve Irwin, died in 2006 after he was pierced by a stingray barb.

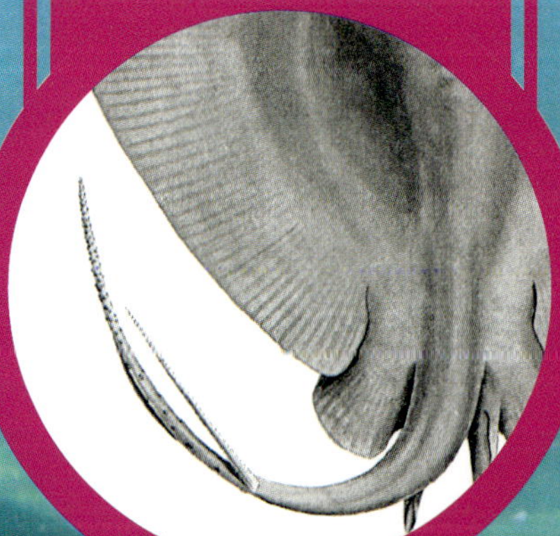

The stingray glides through the ocean, using its delta-shaped flippers like wings. There are many different species, ranging in size from thirty centimetres to two metres wide. They are related to sharks and are cartilaginous fish, which means they do not have hard bones, but instead support their bodies internally with soft cartilage.

WEAPON

The short-tail stingray has stingers and a sharp spike on its long tail. They use their tail as a weapon when they feel threatened.

FACT FILE

Length: up to 2 m wide and 4 m long with tail

Tail: double tail with barbs and a venomous, dagger-like spike up to 30 cm long

Colour: grey and white

Poisonous: stings and piercing can be fatal to humans

Habitat: oceans near southern Australia and Africa

Scientific name: *Dasyatis brevicaudata*

Other name: Smooth stingray

PUFFER FISH

Tetractenos

FACT

In Japan, poisonous puffer fish are prepared by special chefs who know which parts can be eaten. This dangerous meal is called *Fugu*.

The toadfish is Australia's own poisonous puffer fish. There are two types – the smooth and the common toadfish.

The common toadfish does have tiny spikes on its skin, but people who have been poisoned have become ill from eating the fish. The smooth toadfish keeps its spikes under its skin, but it is still poisonous if eaten. They both use the spikes to discourage predators from swallowing them.

Pet dogs who find a dead pufferfish on the beach can die from licking the skin.

FACT

When threatened, they puff up their body to appear bigger, by swallowing water or air.

FACT FILE

Length: 13-15 cm long

Colour: yellow or pale with dark brown spots

Poisonous: poisonous to humans who eat them

Habitat: oceans near southeast Australia in shallow seas and river mouths

Scientific name:
Tetractenos glaber
(smooth toadfish)
Tetractenos hamiltoni
(common toadfish)

SEA SNAKES

About thirty or more types of sea snake live in the seas and oceans around the Australian coast. Sea snakes have evolved to live in the water, but they still need to come to the surface to breathe air.

Some sea snakes look like eels, but you can tell that you have seen a snake if it does not have a fin along its back. Only eels have a dorsal fin. Sea snakes have strong venom and if they feel threatened they can attack people in the water. People fishing with nets are at most risk of a bite from a sea snake if they catch an angry and terrified one in their nets.

FACT

Sea snakes need strong venom so they can quickly immobilise a fish and swallow it before it swims away!

FACT

Sea snakes evolved from land-living snakes, but now they cannot survive long on land.

SEA SNAKE VARIETIES

- **Elegant Sea Snake** (*Hydrophis elegans*)
- **Olive Sea Snake** (*Aipysurus laevis*)
- **Reef Shallows Sea Snake** (*Aipysurus duboisii*), also known as the Dubois' Sea Snake, is one of the most venomous snakes in the world
- **Turtle-headed Sea Snake** (*Emydocephalus annulatus*)
- **Yellow-bellied Sea Snake** (*Hydrophis platurus*)

STONEFISH

Synanceia

There are two types of stonefish that live in Australian seas, and they are both very dangerous. Along its back, the stonefish has spines attached to venom sacs. It is one of the most venomous fish anywhere.

They look like stones or pieces of coral and they sit motionless on the seafloor, sometimes covered in sand. Swimmers who touch one can suffer immediate, intense pain and quickly develop breathing difficulties.

FACT

Stonefish spines are only used against predators, and not for catching food.

FACT FILE

Length: 30 cm long

Colour: mottled brown, grey and red

Poisonous: yes

Habitat: shallow oceans, rock pools and river mouths in warm oceans

Scientific Name:
Synanceia verrucosa
Synanceia horrida

FACT

Stonefish will not swim away if touched and will depend on their poison for protection.

SEA ANEMONE

FACT

In the movie, *Finding Nemo*, the little clownfish lives amongst an anemone's tentacles.

The beautiful sea anemones are related to jellyfish, but they attach themselves to surfaces rather than swimming in the ocean. Anemones have many different shapes, sizes and colours, and they make up a large part of coral reef life.

Anemones have tentacles that can be pulled back into the body for protection. The tentacles have stinging cells that shoot out venom in a tiny spear that can both catch prey and also deter predators.

FACT FILE

Length: colonies can be tiny or very large

Colour: many colours and shapes

Poisonous: yes

Habitat: throughout the world's oceans, with about 40 types in the Great Barrier Reef

FACT

People who keep a sea anemone in a fish tank will be stung if they touch it.

SPONGES

FACT

Natural sponges can be used to wash ourselves in the bath. These are the soft skeletons of sea sponges and do not have sharp spikes.

The sponge is a very ancient type of aquatic animal in a group called Porifera. They may look like a rock or even a plant and are covered in small holes, which they use to filter their food out of the seawater. A piece cut off from a living sponge can grow into a whole new animal.

Touching some sponges, (in particular the bright red fire sponges), can cause a painful rash on human skin.

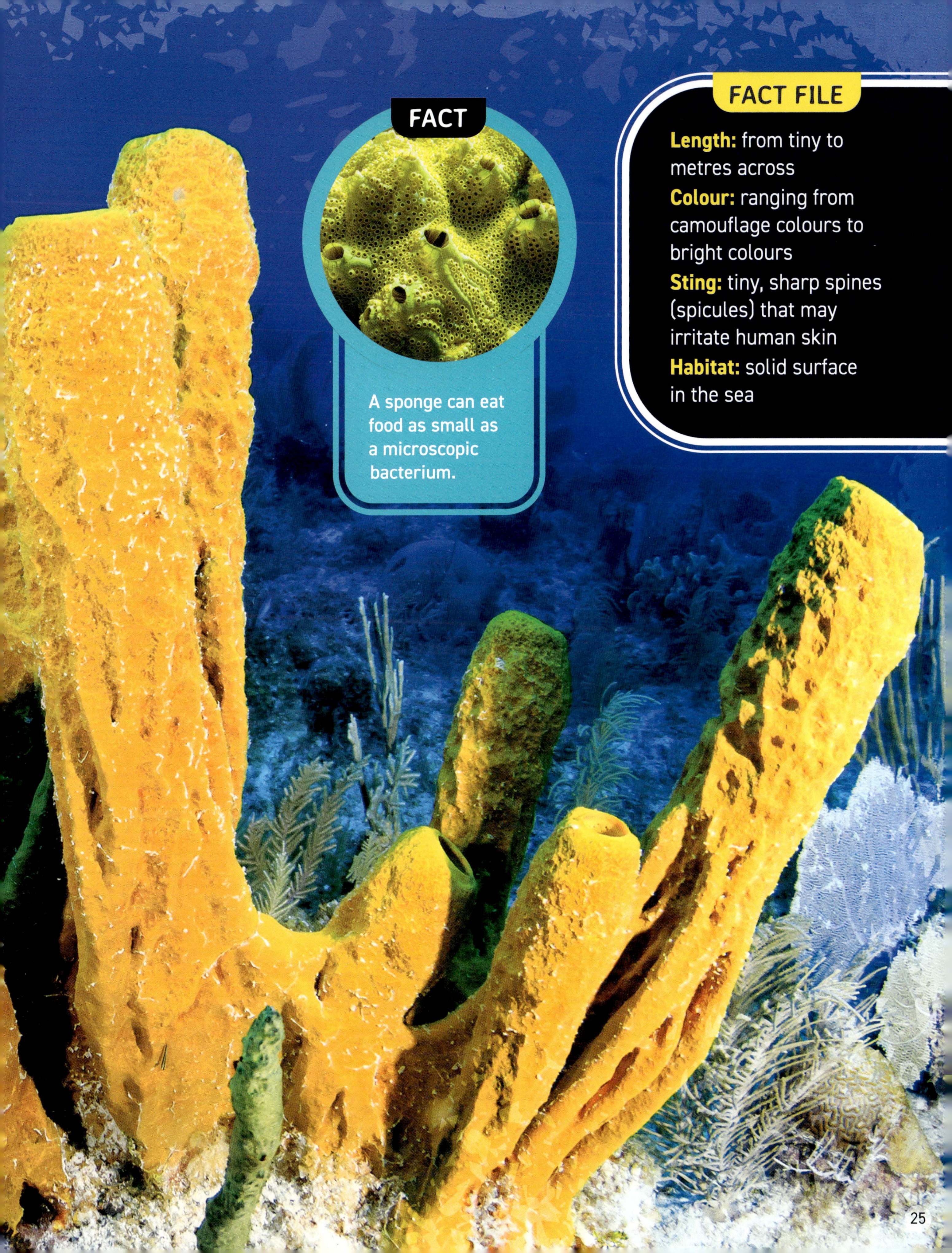

FACT

A sponge can eat food as small as a microscopic bacterium.

FACT FILE

Length: from tiny to metres across

Colour: ranging from camouflage colours to bright colours

Sting: tiny, sharp spines (spicules) that may irritate human skin

Habitat: solid surface in the sea

STINGERS AROUND THE WORLD

ELECTRIC EEL

These eels can produce enough electricity in their skin to give a human a nasty electric shock. They live in South America in the Amazon River region.

SCORPION FISH

These fish have venom-coated spines on their back. Despite this, the fish is often caught by fishers and prepared as a meal.

CATFISH

Catfish are often caught by people fishing. The sharp spines on catfish fins can cause painful stings.

SEA URCHIN

Sea urchins are collected for food by people around the world. Before the sea urchins can be eaten in a meal, the long, sharp spines that they use to protect themselves have to be removed. A spine can stick through a foot or hand, causing an extremely painful injury.

Hydroids are stinging animals that look like plants or feathers growing on top of coral or on rocks on the seafloor. Their bodies are covered in stinging cells.

HOW DANGEROUS ARE THEY?

Creatures in the sea that sting, bite and inject poison have all evolved to have these adaptations for two main purposes. Firstly, they need to kill food, and secondly, they need to protect themselves from becoming food for a predator.

People who enjoy swimming and diving in the sea are likely to come into contact with poison from one of these creatures at some time. The results can be mild and annoying, or deadly.

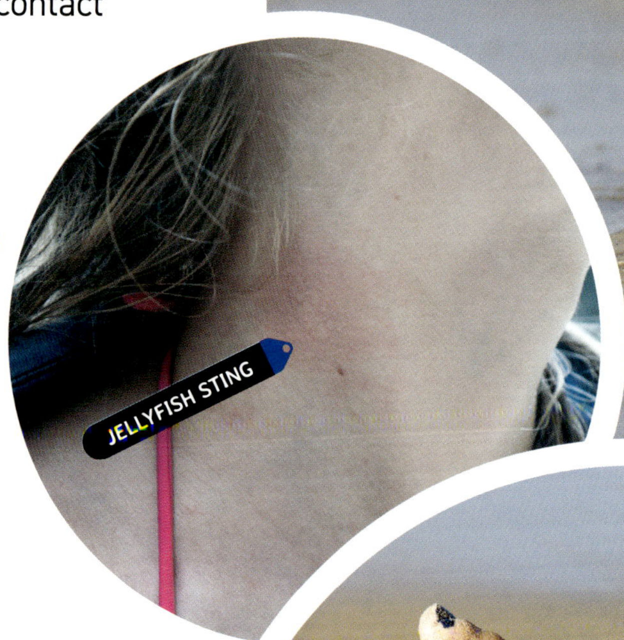

Here are some of the effects these poisons can have on humans:

- Pain at the site of the sting
- Muscle pain throughout the body
- Difficulty breathing
- Fever
- Vomiting
- Sweating
- Confusion
- Paralysis
- Fainting
- Death

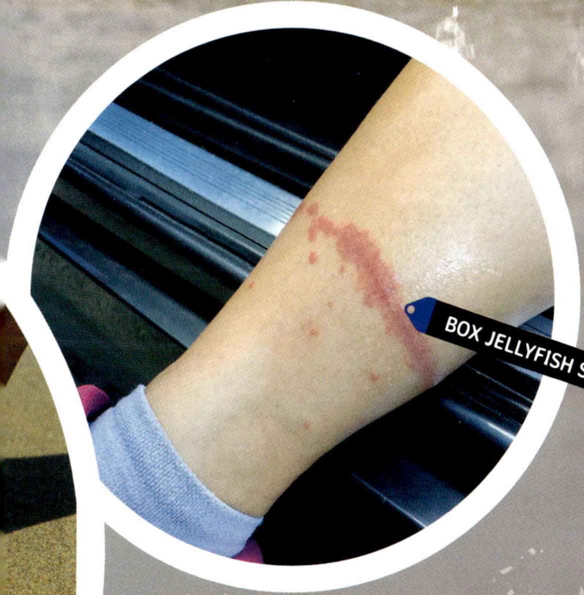

BOX JELLYFISH STING INJURY

WARNING

Coastlines that have a lot of stingers will often display warning signs.

SAFETY IN THE OCEAN

Wear a wetsuit or clothing that covers the skin.

Wear goggles.

Swim at patrolled beaches where the lifeguards can help in the event of an emergency.

Be aware that you share the water with billions of other creatures.

GLOSSARY

Avoid ocean water during the 'stinger season' in Australia's north.

Shark Word List

cartilaginous	made of soft cartilage
crustaceans	prawns, crabs, lobsters
delta-shaped	shaped like a letter D
mollusc	animal group that includes snails, mussels and octopuses
mottled	mixed colours and patterns
nausea	feeling like vomiting
nematocyst	tiny capsule that holds stinging barbs
sac	pouch or bag-like structure
sense of impending doom	feeling that something very bad is about to happen
toxin	poison
translucent	letting some light through
venom	poison that is injected

Keep yourself and pets away from dead stinging animals on the beach.

Don't poke at creatures in rock pools or when diving or snorkelling.

INDEX

catfish 27
electric eel 26
Fugu 16
Great Barrier Reef 5, 23
hydroid 27
Irwin, Steve 14
pets 16, 31
Porifera 24
Portuguese Man o' War 8
rock pools 6, 21
scorpion fish 26
sea urchin 27
smooth stingray 15
spicule 25
stinger season 12, 31
toadfish 16, 17